PAPERBACK TEARS: The Journey Begins Now…

Poetry: Cathleen Jo Faruque

Photography: Amy Folse

First Printing

ISBN-13: 978-1461102458

ISBN-10: 1461102456

DEDICATION

This book is dedicated to the people who have influenced our lives directly, indirectly, inadvertently, consciously, purposefully, insidiously, inconspicuously, modestly, wholeheartedly, and completely. Who can honestly tell which of the paths we will take in this life? We believe we come to this Earth for a reason and that there is no chance meeting in life. Each of us influences one and other – sometimes significantly, sometimes ever so slightly, and other times a meeting may appear to have no meaning at all – later to realize the opportunity, however short, was one of the most important encounters of all.

May we be so fortunate to have a chance encounter one day!

Love and Peace,

Cathy and Amy

ABOUT THE AUTHORS:

Cathy Faruque and Amy Folse have been lifelong friends. Starting from their primary school days to present, Cathy and Amy have continued to share their passion for expression through the art of poetry and photography. This book is but a small sample of their efforts to share their passion with others. We acknowledge that often fact is stranger than fiction. However, any resemblance to anything or person was entirely accidental and wholly coincidental.

Light of the Night

Northern light beauty
Caress the moon beams
Cascade to the skies
Twinkling night stars.

Northern light beauty
Captures the end of day
Ever the watchful
Stream of lights flush.

Colors brighten that northern sky
Reminders that winter
Is not far by.

North light beauty
To behold
Telling a story only
The night secrets hold.

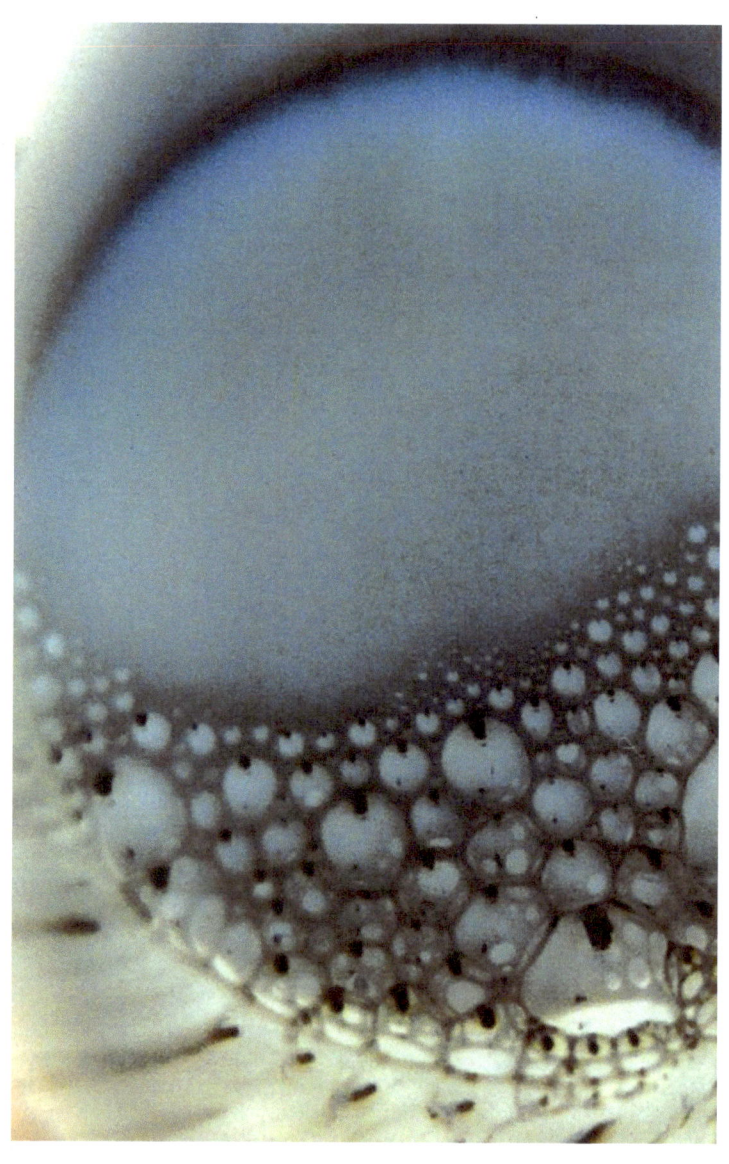

Nights of Thunder

Slumber disrupted
Bursting forth with a
F
  L
    A
      S
        H
Swift as the momentum
of darkness –
Is it truth?
Through deafening rumble
of remote thunder
Affirmation is heard
Where display is no more,
hearing takes over.
D
  A
    N
  C
      I
  N
  G
translucent drops
burst upon the roof top,
shimmy down the rain pipe
S
    P
        L
        A
     S
H
Upon the window pane
And descend to the
Soft crusted earth.

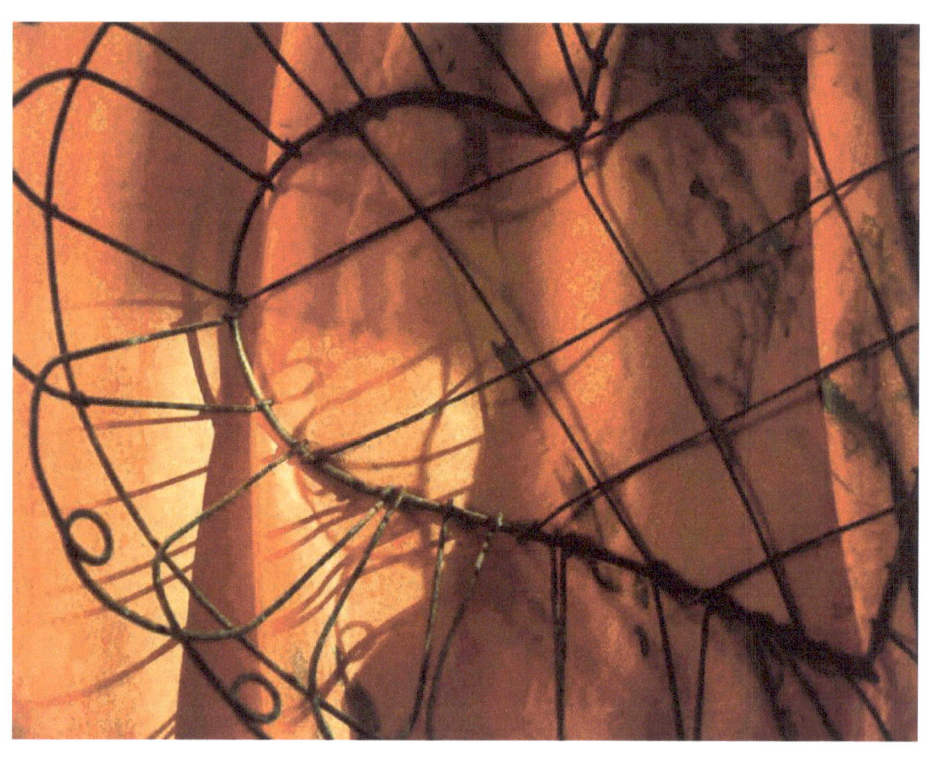

Divine Love

The Path to the Divine can be found through
Love, Mercy, Compassion, and Understanding
Oh Swami, enlighten us to bridge the gaps
Eradicate the imperceptible and translucent impediments
That produces supremacy, brutality, and cruelty in our world!

The message of the Divine is more potent than any vindication
Collectively we can unearth exposition
To eradicate poverty, suffering, and human tyranny
We can break the vicious cycle
Building bridges instead of walls

A soul in search of the Divine's love
Can overcome any adversary
The ears ready to heed the Divine's voice
Can vanquish all evil

Embrace your brother
Welcome your sister
Bring illumination and optimism to humankind
Problems found from inside
Find the solutions from within

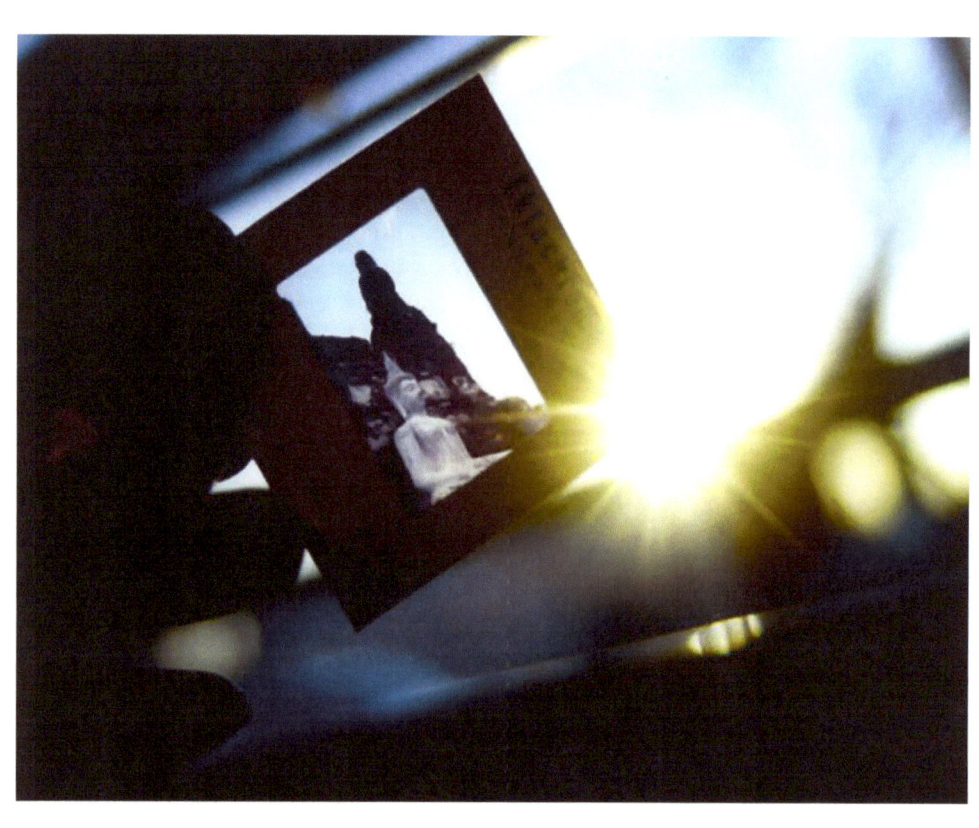

Frozen Interlude

Wind chill minus 20
fingers frozen to the bone
toes feel like ice crystals forming
nose red as a cherry
no hope for tomorrow
weather to be the same
through Saturday

I hate winter
Summer where are you?
When will this end?

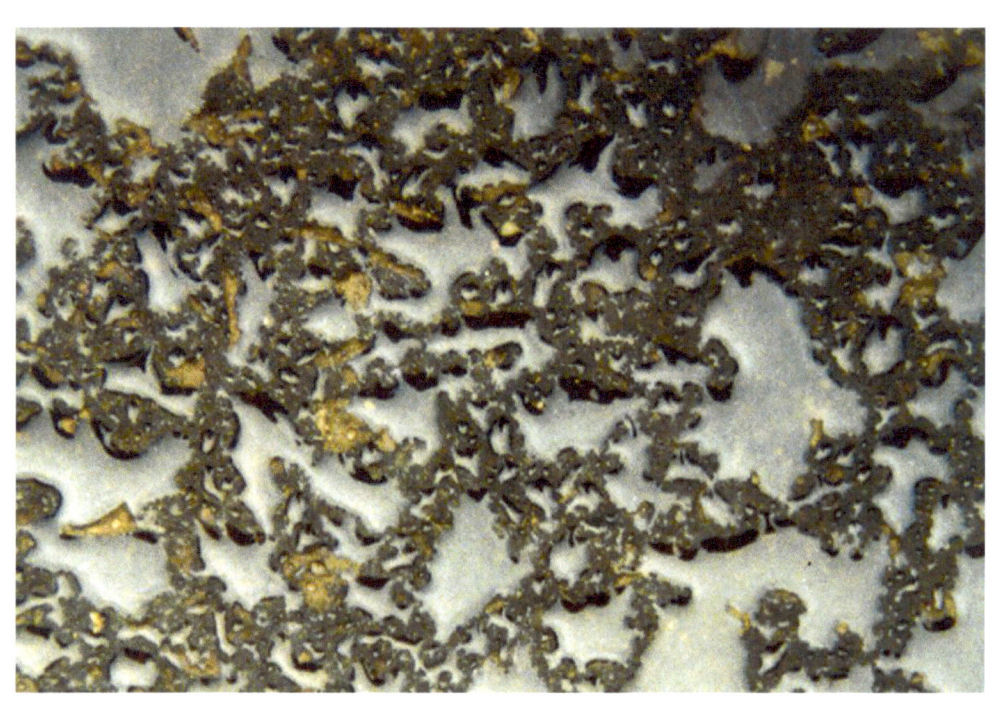

12

Stillness

Stillness of night
ever present at my window.
Keep silent the stars
'ere the wind hears their song.

Canopy of clouds
drift past like a curtain.
The moon beams that glow
are new to the night.

Stillness of night
stays upon my window.
The rays of starlight
revealed in the grass.

Gone are the cares of
stars in the twilight.
No sadness lies here in
the darkness of night.

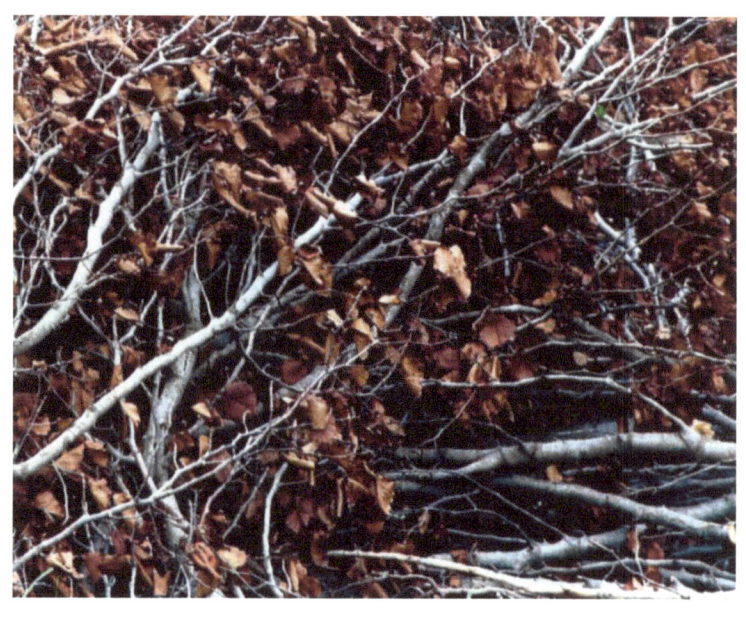

14

Summer Blossoms

Whispering willows
Gentle breeze
Cool winds across
Floating among the tree leaves.
Crickets gently
Call out to the night
As the feel of rain
Creates a stirring chill
Pansies prepare for
A night to sleep
Waiting for morning
To begin summer's bloom.
Whispering winds
Sing gentle words
Across my window pane
In the gentle summer eve

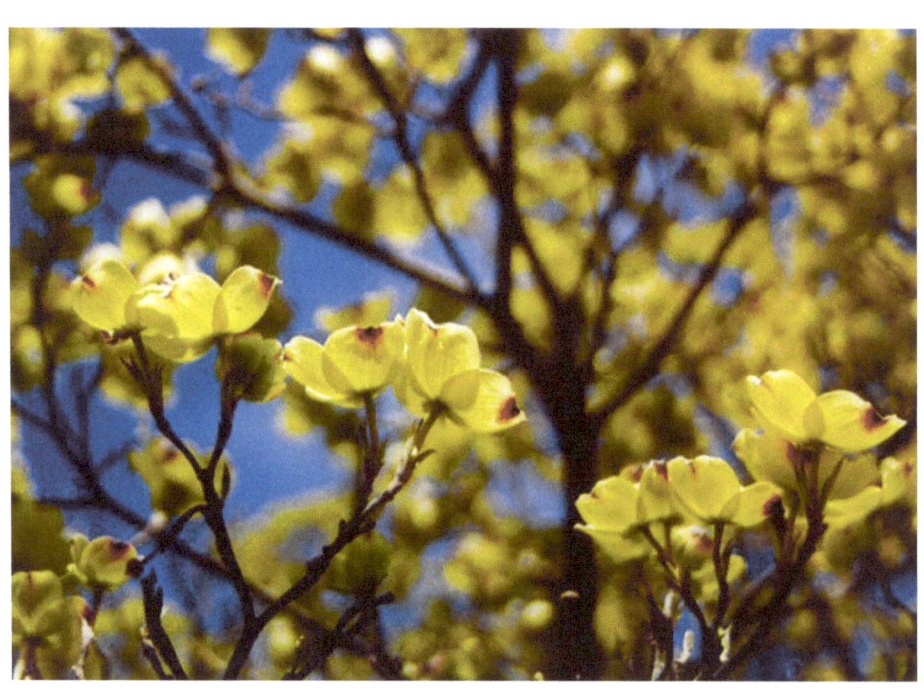

Faith

Contained by the heart
Wrapped securely
Inside,
The mind holds the
Key to the
Contents within.

Faith is the remedy
To the question
Asked from above,
Credence in the possessor
Of simplicity
Is key.

Exonerate those who
Enter with impudent
Humility.
But stand for the
Truth and cast
Misgivings aside.

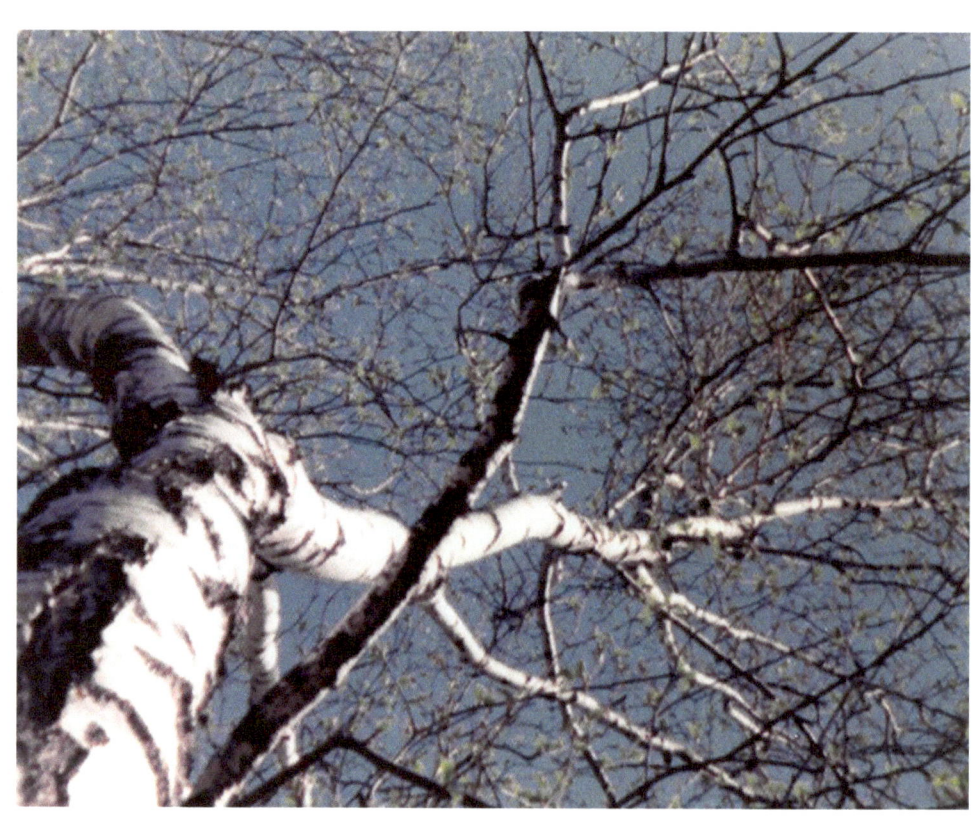

18

Winterlude

Blasts of blowing chill
Freezing droplets of water
On my windowpane.

Snow drifts across
The dunes of pure white
In neighboring yards.

Winter is upon
The doorstep and
Awaits the open door.

The winds moan
Creaking doors
And rattling windows.

Winter has arrived.

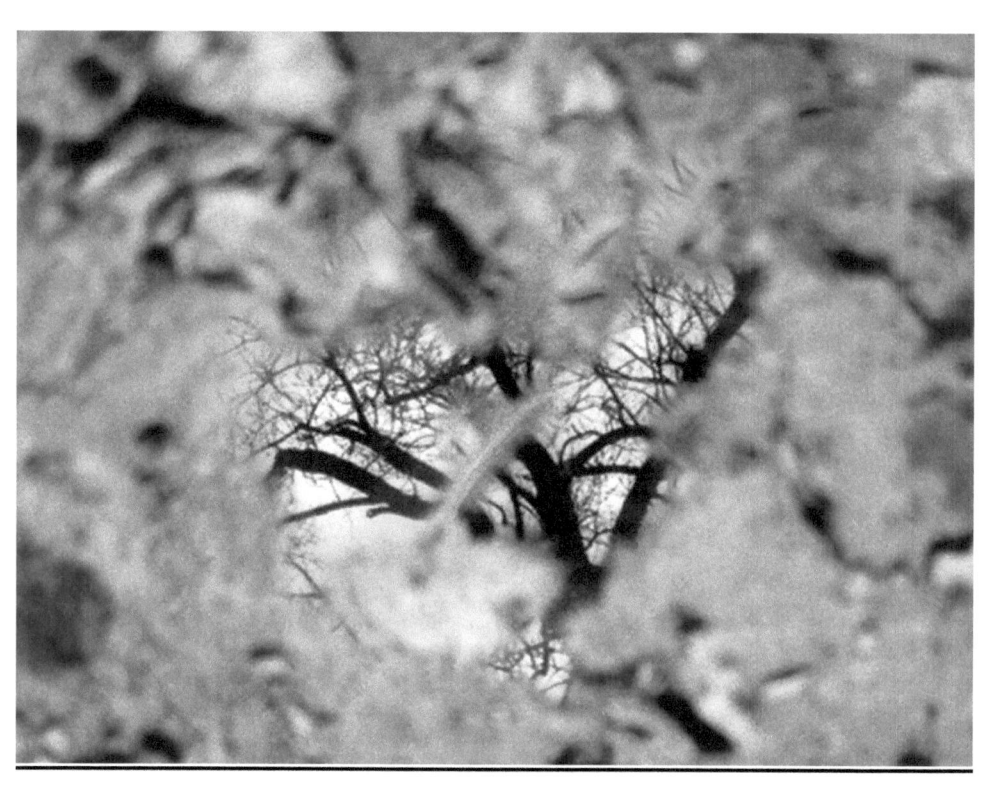

Poetry is Vindictive

Poetry is a flowery art
Formations that describe
Reflections of the
Contempt
One has for
Convention
And contemporary
Ideas
That are expressed
In such a manner
As to fool the
Reader into
Believing there
Must be truth
In the written word.

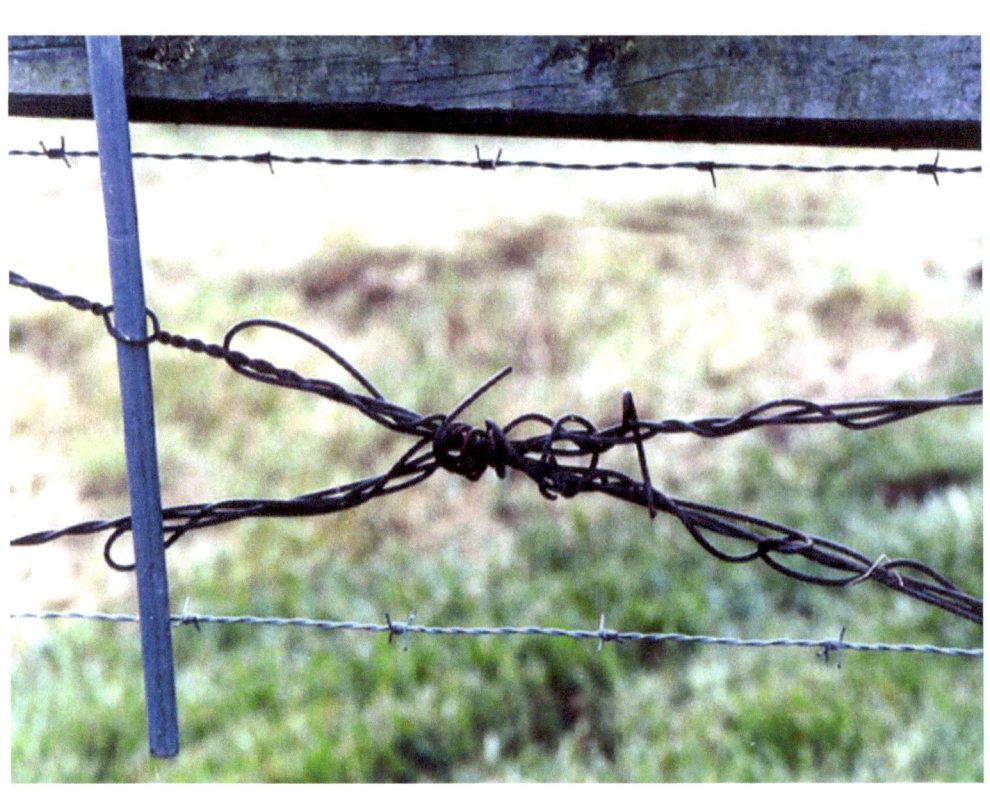

The Window

Streaks of yellow, gold, red and green
Peaking through sun soaked windows.
Bird songs flow throughout
Ever mindful of the day
Peaking through sun streaked windows.

The cat dances along the window's ledge
Wishing he were outside
Devouring the birds intently watched
The day through his perch on the window
Waiting for the sign that the door
Will somehow magically open.

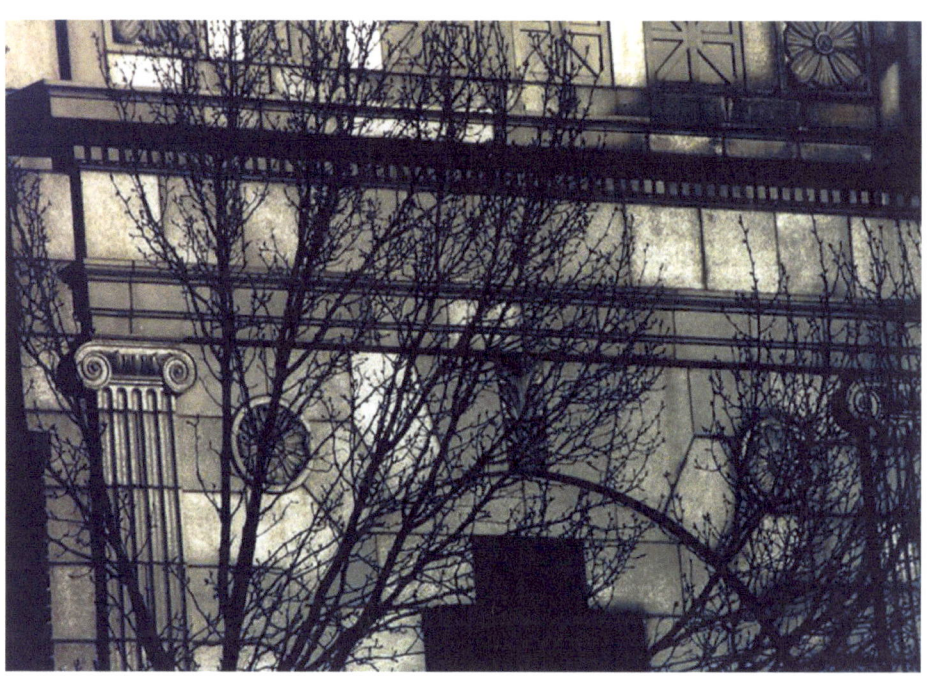

Summer Rain

The torrential rains amid

bright flashes of light

loud claps of thunder

Water pools soak the ground

eternal mud

awaits the gardener

Captives indoors like

impatient children

hope for a show of sun

Cool and moist

damp to the core

chilled to the bone

Mind over matter

No hope for the summer

Perhaps autumn will come soon.

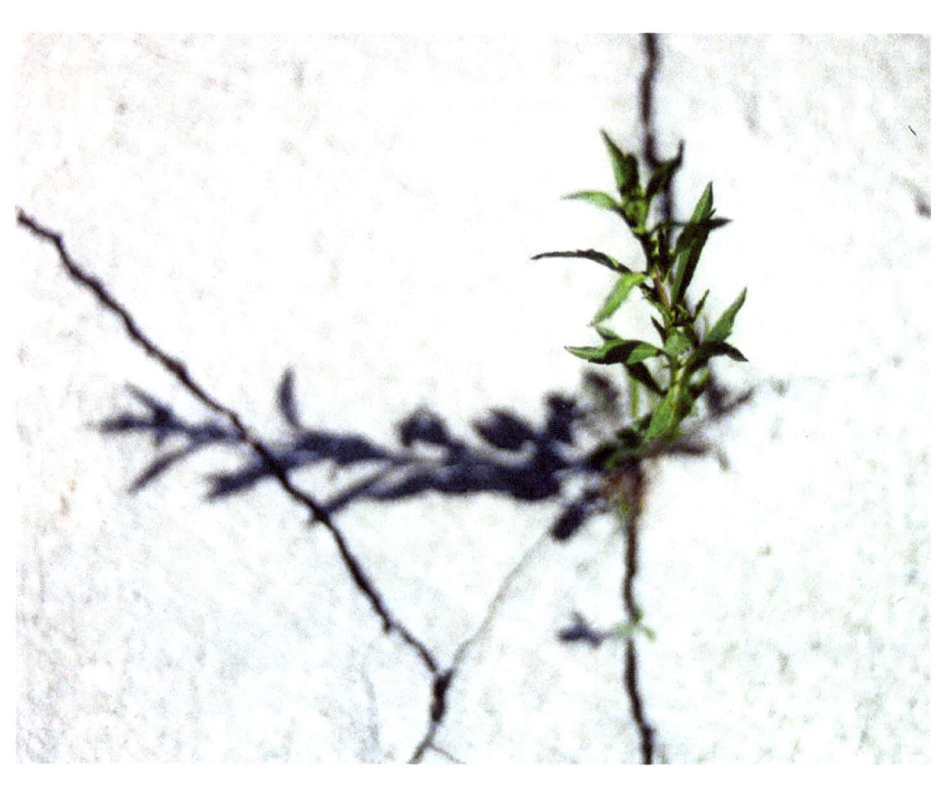

Time Passes

Across the winter skies all the days are passing.
How was I to know that it was time for us to go.
For the winter has come and yet I am still dreaming
Being close to you with no care for the time.
Who knows where the time goes?
Who knows how our love grows?

Soft deserted shores, so far from your love from me
I know your love is leaving me.
How could I know it was time to go?
But I can still feel you and I have no thought of leaving you,
I have no thought of time.
Who knows where the time goes?
Who knows how our love grows?

I was so alone, while your love was near to me.
I need for you to say the words, but it is time for me to go.
So harsh the storms of winter that all the birds fly away
Yet I have fear of the time.
Who knows where the time goes?
Who knows how our love grows?

I feel soft and warm your heart near to me
I need to know love is shared, across the lonesome sky
Alone the winter days pass by.
Yet I feel no thought for the time.
Who knows where the time goes?
Who knows how our love grows?

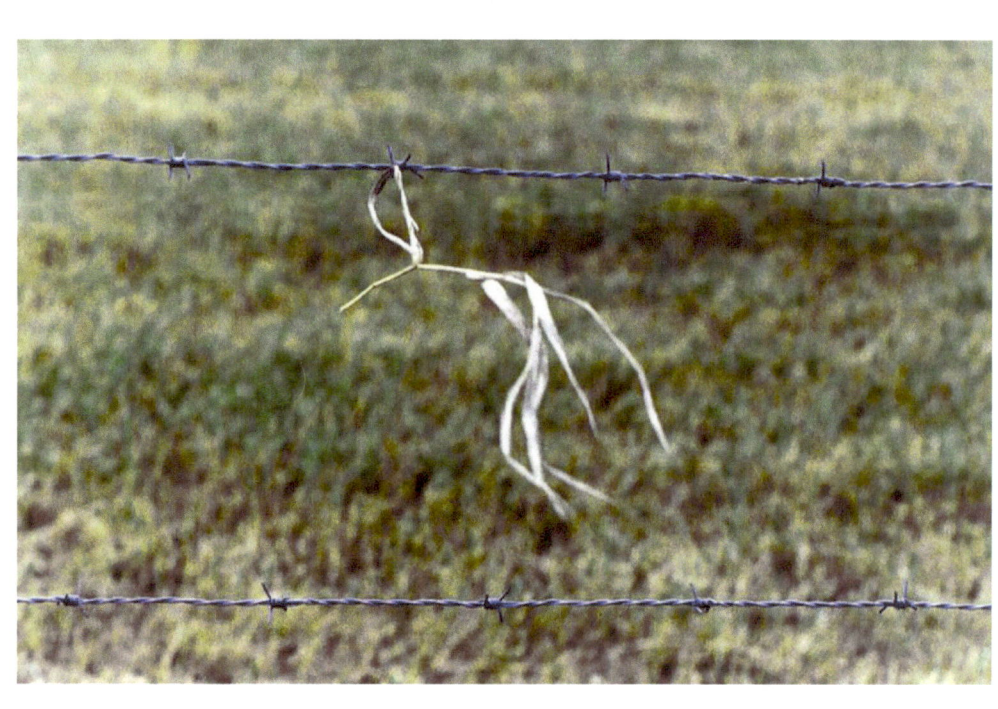

28

Solitude

My heart beats only for you
for as long as you want me
my wandering heart is
lost in painful memories of you
only hopeful to be near you.
Can my love sustain you
or will you find someone new?
Days pass so long and lonely
without you here.
Each day is the same as
the day before.
Waiting for you
hoping to hold you
to keep you
for a while.

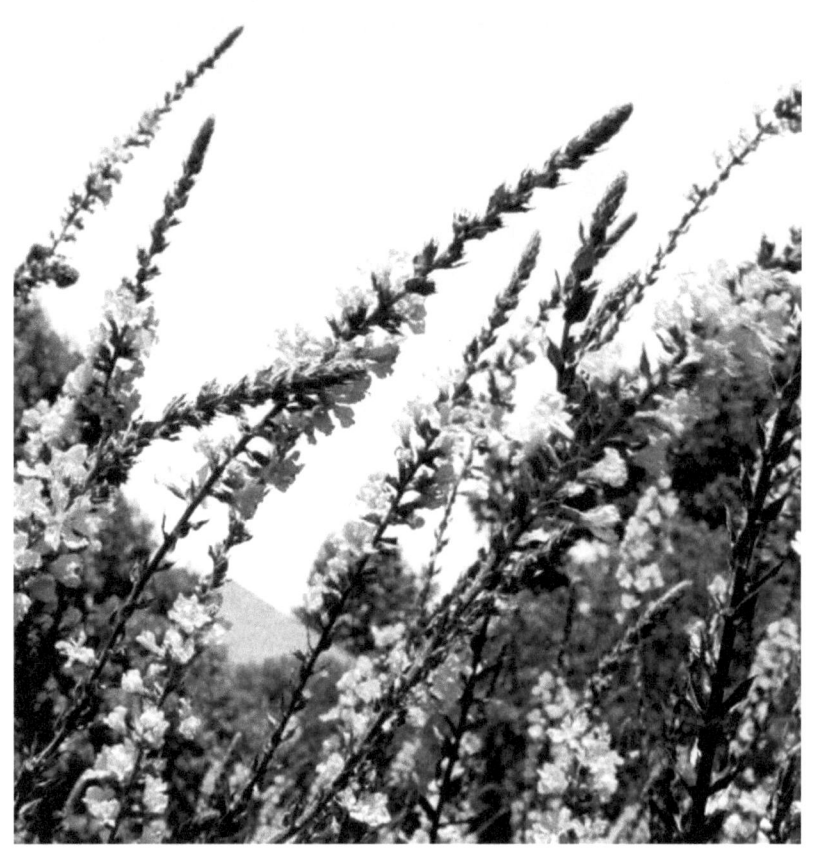

Ice Moon

Ice Moon connect and touch
Cold and unattainable reach
Triumphantly glow to Earth in
Sweet perigee
Making the brilliant sphere
Bigger, brighter, perpetual
Dancing in the black liquid sky.
Dreaming of the distance
From the Ice Moon to
Your heart.
Hanging on to the night
When your touch converges
And is attainable on this
Icy winter night.
Clandestine moments that transpire
An Ice Moon and transparent breath.
Draw near to welcome me
You are the Ice Moon.
Be as attainable as the limits of
Universe and time.
Conceal not your secrets
But share your wispy light
Cast a glow over the frozen
Wasteland of lake and trees.
Embrace the stars in the wintery sky.
Tangle in the night with
Venus and Mars.
Be not overshadowed by eclipse,
Cloud, rain, or snow.
Share the mysteries of this icy night
And hold me in your gentle embrace.

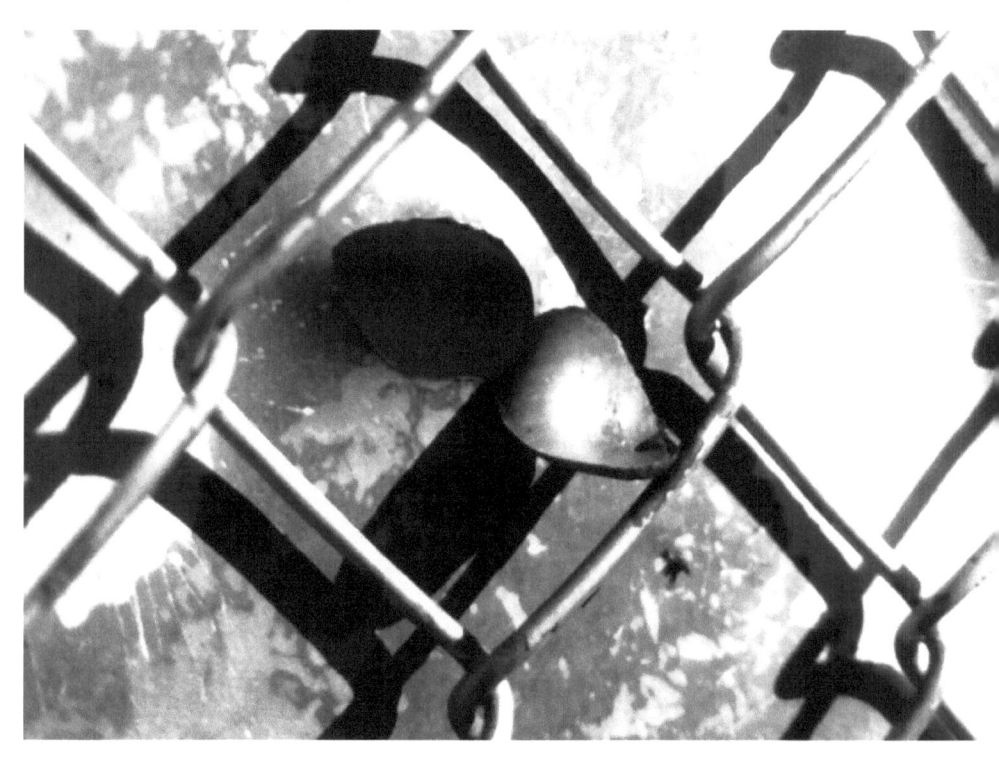

Pass Slowly This Night

Rickshaw Wallah please pass slowly this night
No rush to our destination for now.
Riding in cramped quarter
Stars twinkle delight
Quarter moon hails in black sky
Bells tinkle their magical tune
Riders balanced embrace
Whispers in the twilight
Herald promises unspoken.
Misunderstood perhaps
Language passes slowly as time passes quick.
Two riders in tune to the sounds of the street.
Hold quickly, laugh heartily,
drink softly the memory.
Capture this moment and keep it intact
Let not one moment be forgotten
Let not one second pass in neglect.
12 23 09
143
369
44
08 18 09
All are memories of time.
Pass slowly dear Wallah
No need to take haste
the destination arrives all too soon
and unleashes the embrace...

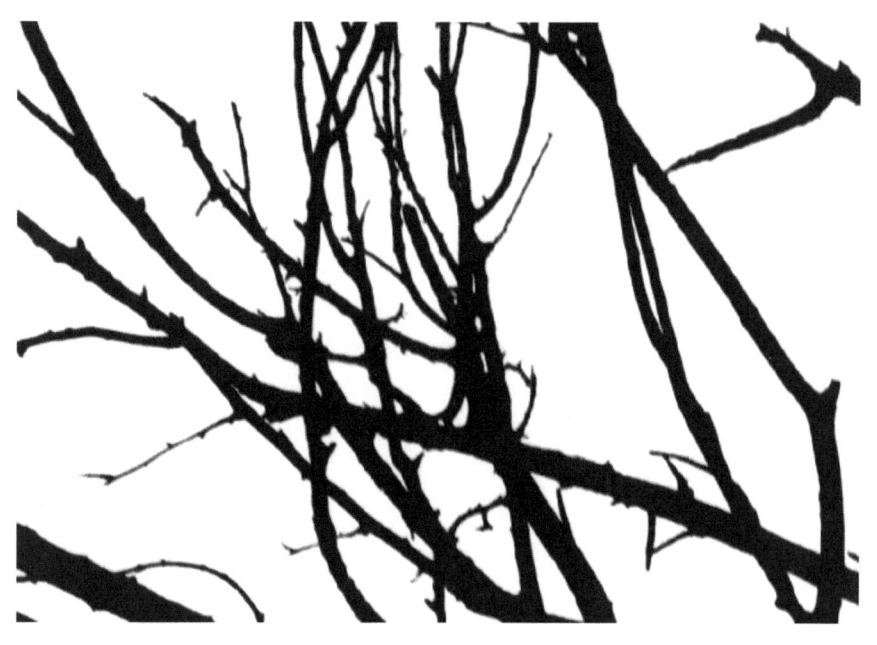

Sentiment

Beautiful liquid pools of black
Deeply eternal
Vast as the universe
Embedded in your eyes.
Countless stories
Told through unmoving lips
Endearing tilt gleaming
Bursting form of memories
Forgotten long ago.
Beaming with knowledge of
What was
What is
What will be.
Cast forever in the depth
of beautiful liquid pools of black
deeply eternal
vast as the universe
embedded in your eyes.

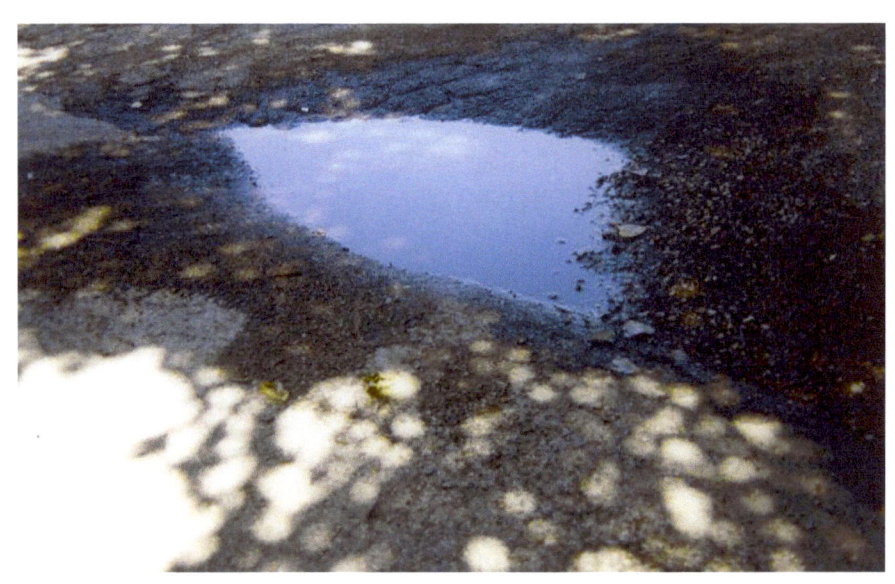

Cold Hard Rain

I listen to the sounds of the rain
outside my window
bitter
sweetly cold
paced rhythms
blue on blue
iced solitude.
Like my heart
cold as ice
on a wintery
day.
No reprieve
No answer
No reason
Only silence in
bitter
sweetly cold
blue on blue
rain.
October rains
chill to the bone
like my heart
chilled to the
core.
Little hope for thaw
perhaps
when spring comes.

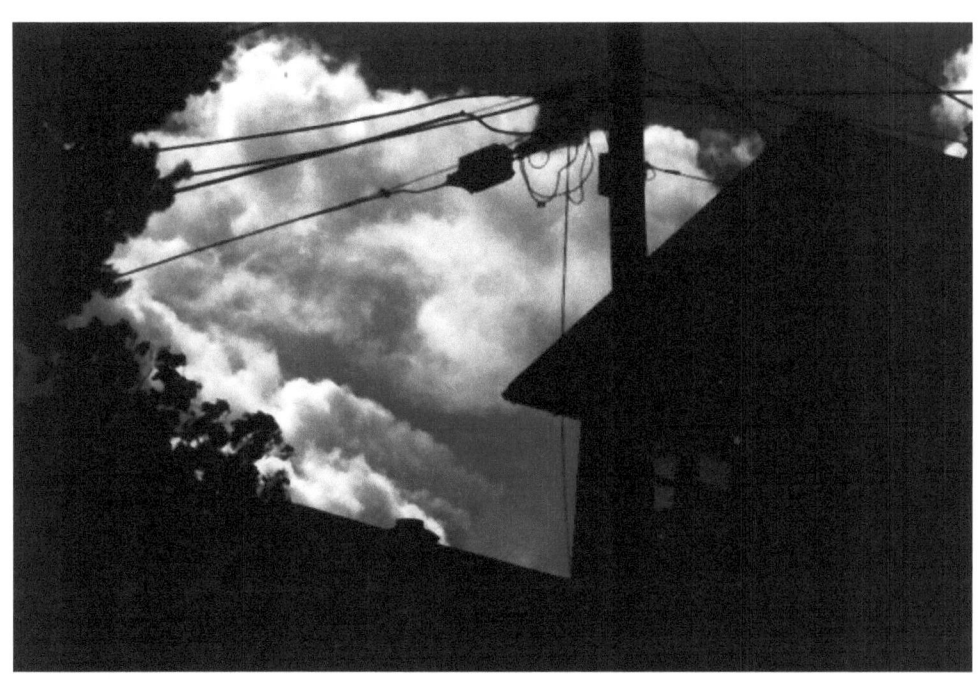

Song for Souls

I listen to the words
To the words of my soul
My soul takes me where
My heart wants to go.
Shaded memories of
A place that my mind
Seeks to a half opened window
In the shadows of your soul.
As I gaze upon the setting sun
A slow dance of burning embers
Burns a thirst in me that cannot be won.
Where souls can hinder as
Two minds that are one
The eyes speak as ageless and
The time is none.
What manner is the dance
We play?
Where will the last scene
In the stage be played?
The words of my soul ring true
My heart sings a song
That only is heard by you.
How shall we pass the
Time and space
That only the soul can trace

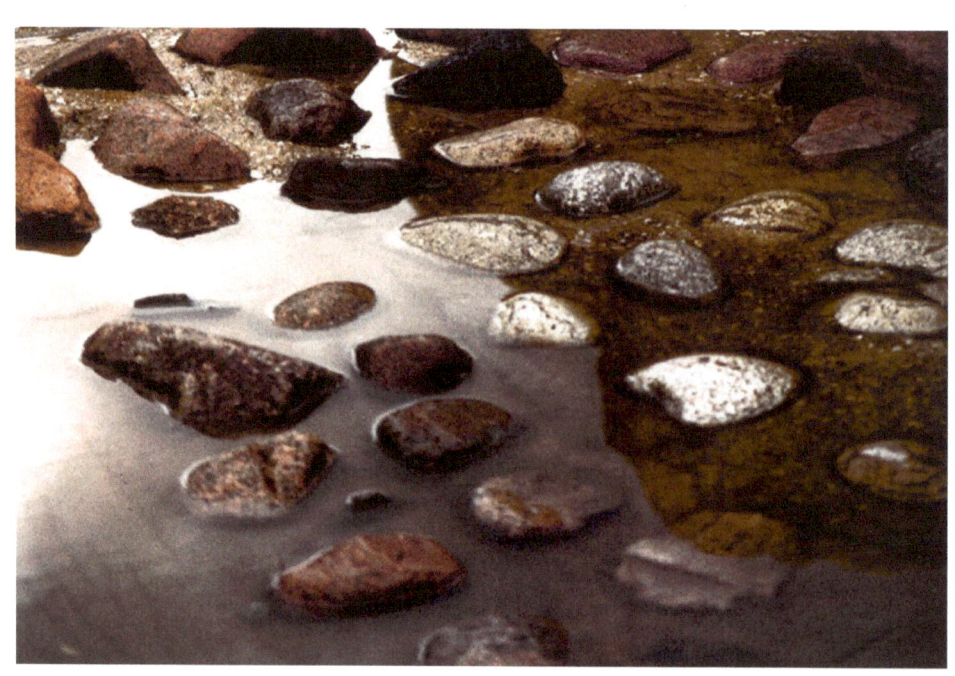

Wakeful Sleep

Taunt me with your smile
Tease me with your laugh
Coax me with your eyes
Catch me with your heart.
Foolishly caught in the
great web of
time.
Catching me like the
north west winds that
throw wicked waves
on the water's edge.
What a tangle
What a torment.
Why bring out
what was peacefully sleeping
to succumb to desire
never quenched,
Like a thirst never
satisfied
As the ripples of
memory
entice me ever
farther and nearer
to you.

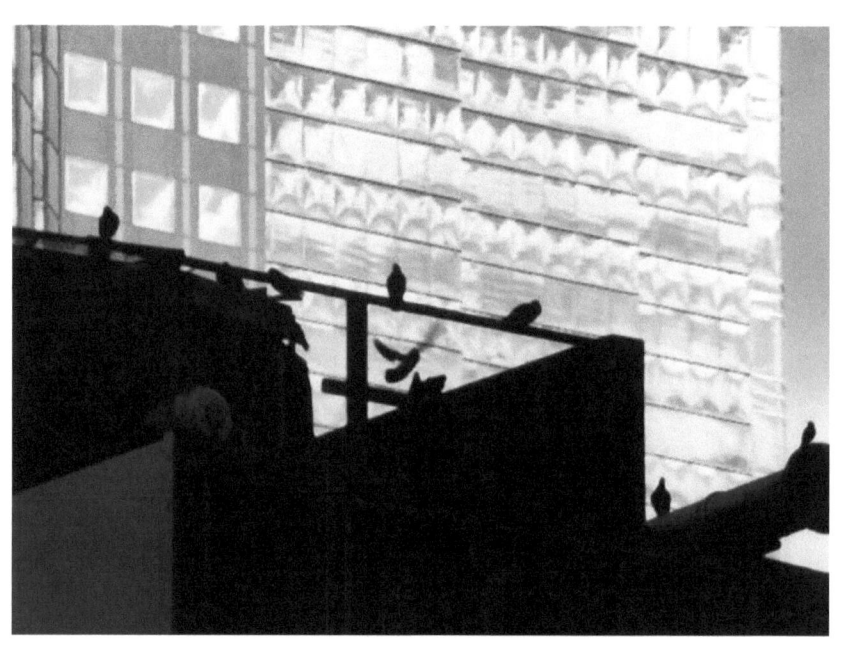

Breathing

Breathing
Slowly heart beat
Increased
By thoughts of you
Embraced in
Memory.
Time is a
Wicked game.
Memories an
Agony for
A tormented soul
Searching for you.
Lost by wicked
Time
Iniquitous memories
Desires
Yearning
Desires.
Gone astray by time
Captured in this body
Imprisoned in this heart
Tortured in this mind
Tormented in this soul.

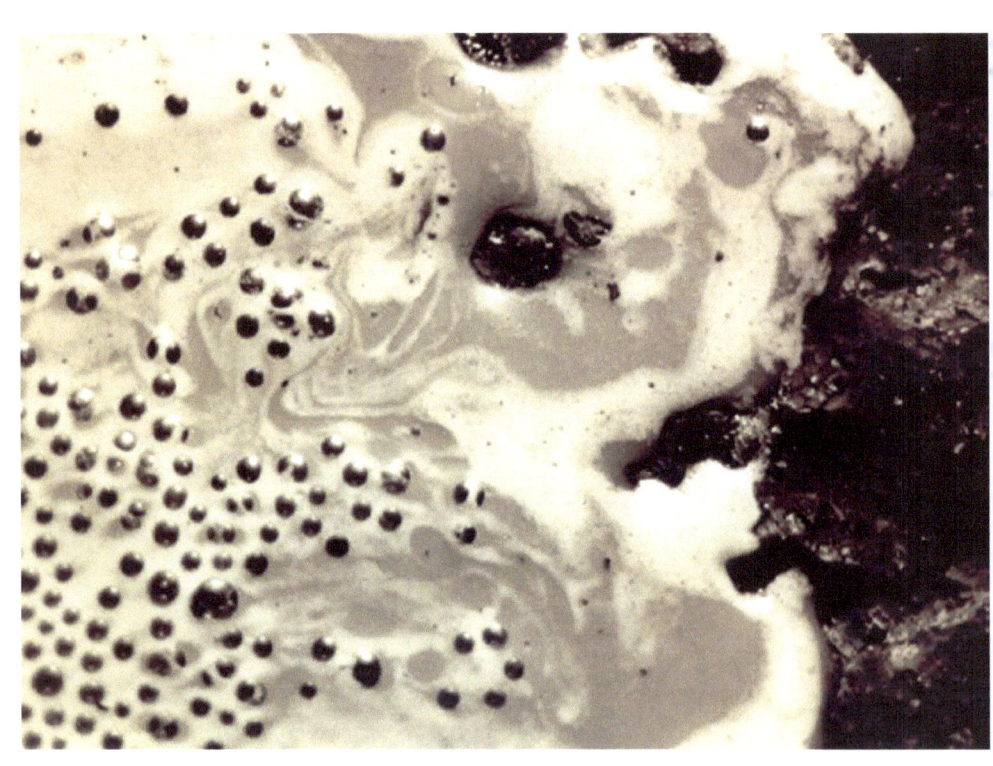

Lonely Night

Half moon casting shimmering
Glows through hazy clouds
Stars shining brightly on a summer evening
A lone plane passes in slow descent.
I wish to be on that plane
But it doesn't go to the place I need to be.
It merely is a symbol
A memory of travel once made
Time lost
Gazing in the cool evening sky
Makes me wonder
Where you are now
A day of bright bursting sunshine
High heat
Humidity
Chance of rain with little doubt
For it is the rainy season now
Or so I have been told.
Seems the dry spell makes it
All so unreal in its own way.
A path that leads to only daydreams
Possibilities
What if
what if
what if?
But there is only now
There is only here
There is only this
Lonely night.

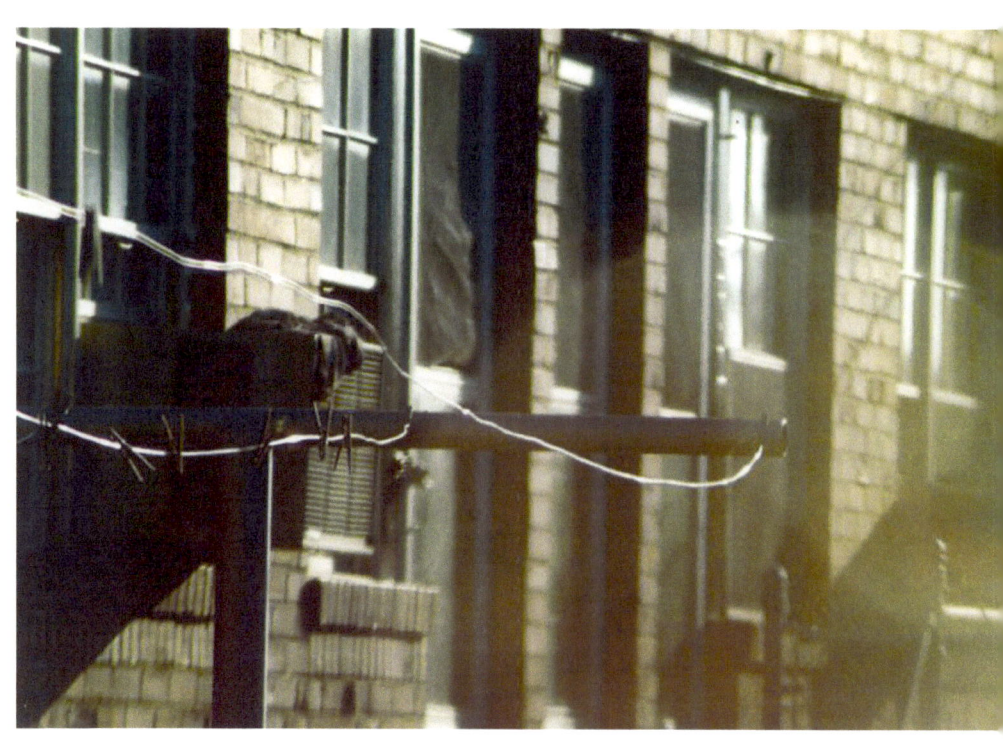

Twilight

In the twilight
By the moonlight
Under star light
Sensing dawn's light
You are nearby
Approaching heart's light
Safety keeping in
Your memory
Your rhythmic breathing
Is breathtaking
Encroaching sadness
Without ending
I know you hear me
When I whisper
Your name in heart's breath
Without speaking
Your senses reeling
Your mind excelling
As I wonder
Upon the moon's light
Will you ever be forgotten
Will you ever be remembered
Will our memories be entwined
Will we know when time has ended
In the twilight
By the moonlight
Under star light
Sensing dawn's light.

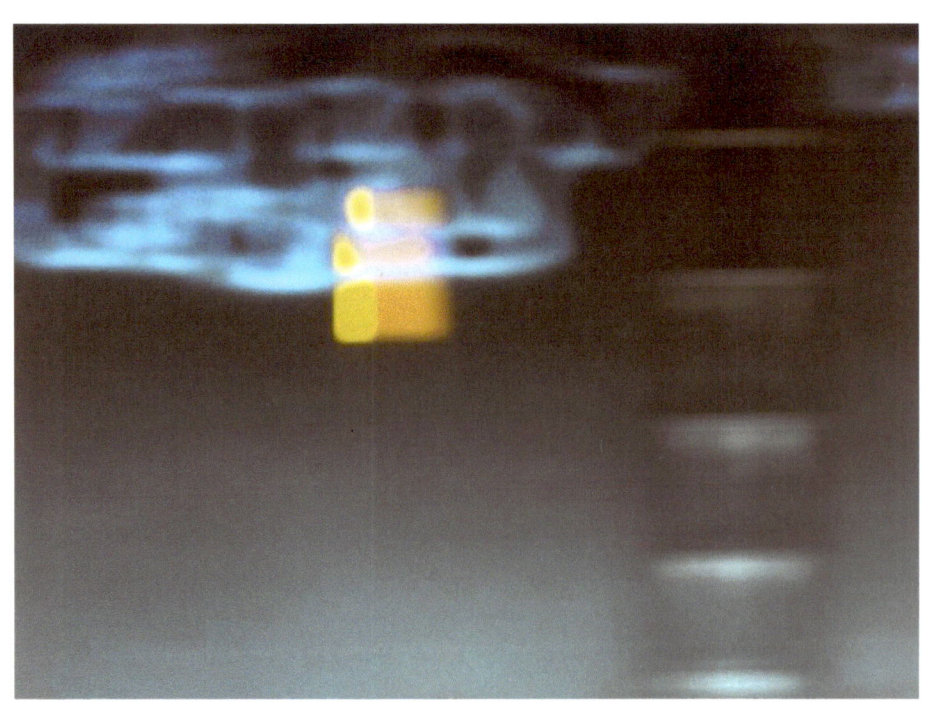

Summer Moon

Beneath the magnificent shimmer of a full moon
On a balmy summer evening in June
With the sweet scent of lilies in the air
We rode on the rickshaw so fair
The moonlight on the water
Shown brightly through the trees
This eternal memory came drifting
Along with the tender breeze
We rode on the eclipse of the moonshine
Sharing with each other a moment so fine.
So if you see the next gleam of full moon
Rising full in the month of June
With the smell sweet trace of lilies in the air
Please remember the time we shared
Watching the moonlight on the water
Shining through the trees
And hear the melody come drifting
On the a warm summer breeze
Oh united to the moment
Remembering that night
And ride once again on the rickshaw
In the summer during the full of the moon.

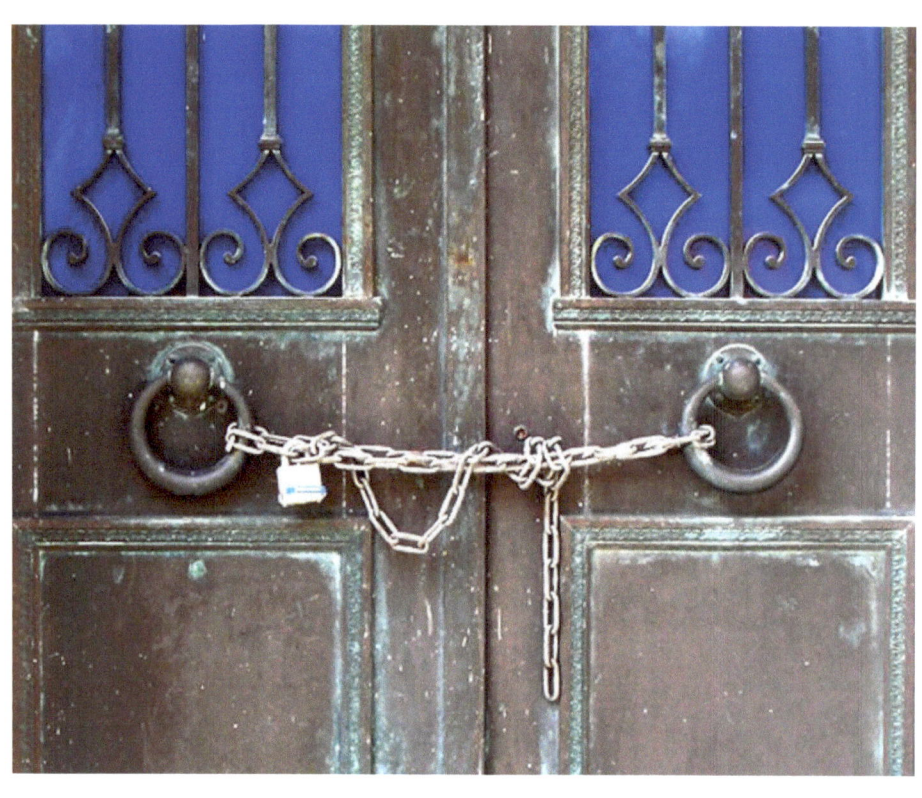

Monday Morning Overhaul

The simplifying
Of a complicated
Structure,
Be it a
Physical or
Psychological
Being that
Evolves
Around the senses
In relation to
The human species,
Can cause
The draining
Of a totality
Of functioning.
It is with
The utmost of care
That I try to
Simplify
You.

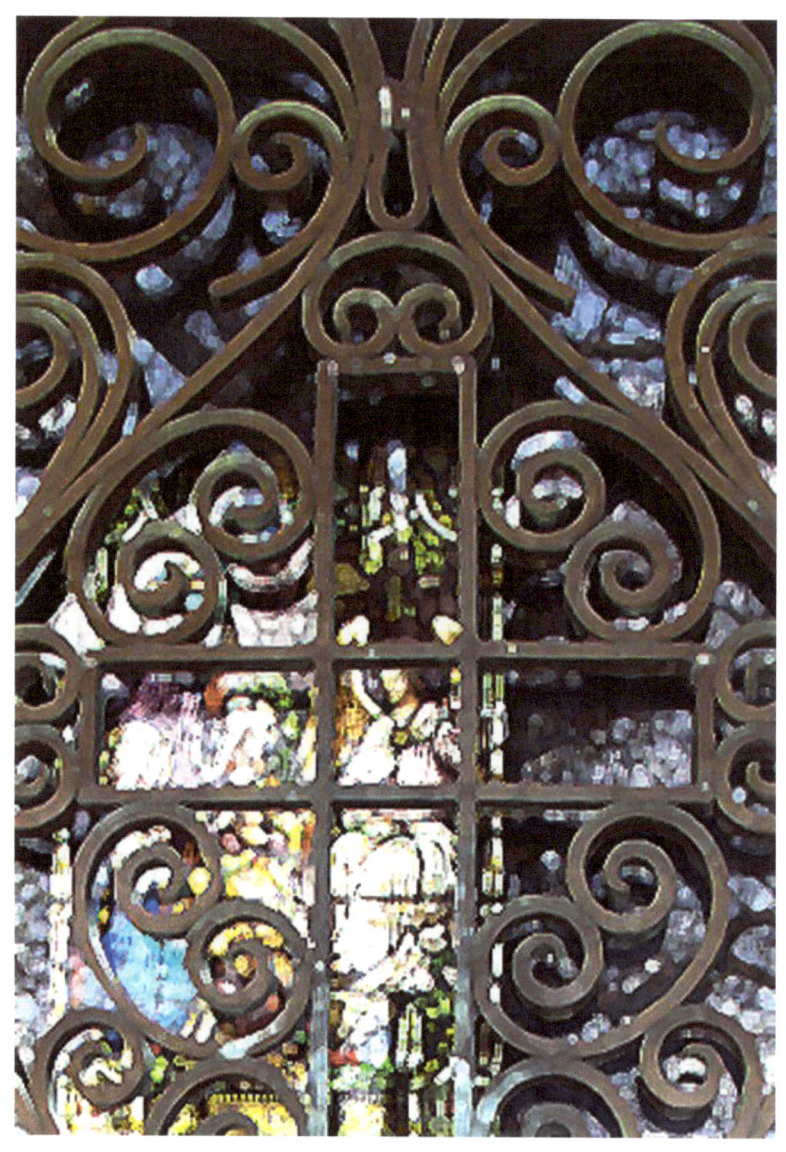

Tears

Tear drop
Softly
Down
The soft
Pink cheek.
Followed by
Another
In the
Hollows of
A blue mass
Of tissue.
Gently
It falls
Until it
Hits the lips
And salt
Tastefully
Caresses the
Flesh
Until it
Encompasses
A world
Lacking of care.

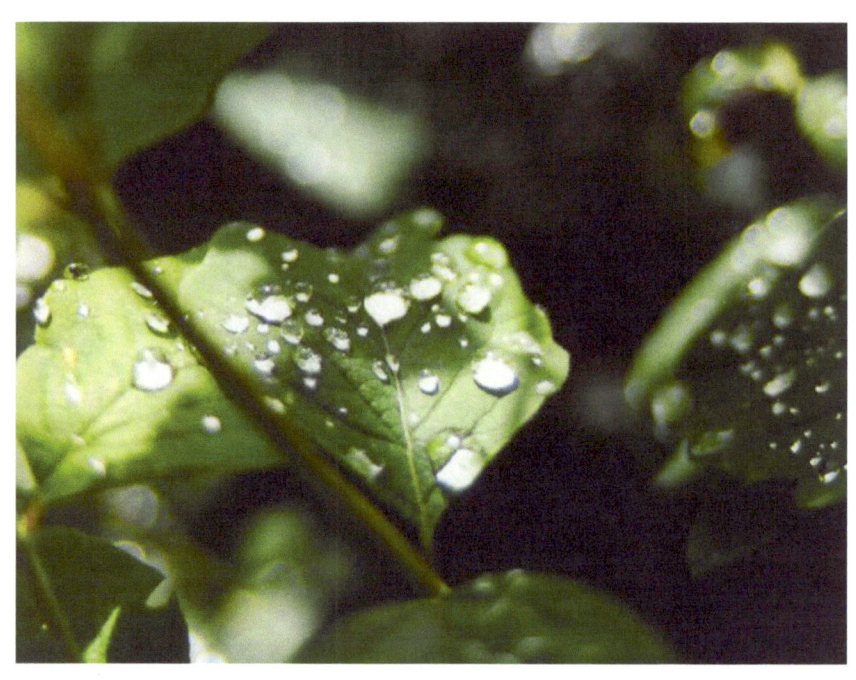

Showers Are Not A Cure

I took a shower
But
Still your smell
Lingers,
As your taste
Tingles…
How could I ever…
But it is
History now,
Yet I long for…
If ever I wanted…
I don't understand
And where does it go
From here?
As the petal is
Just a part of
The flower,
So am I just a
Lamented part
Without you.

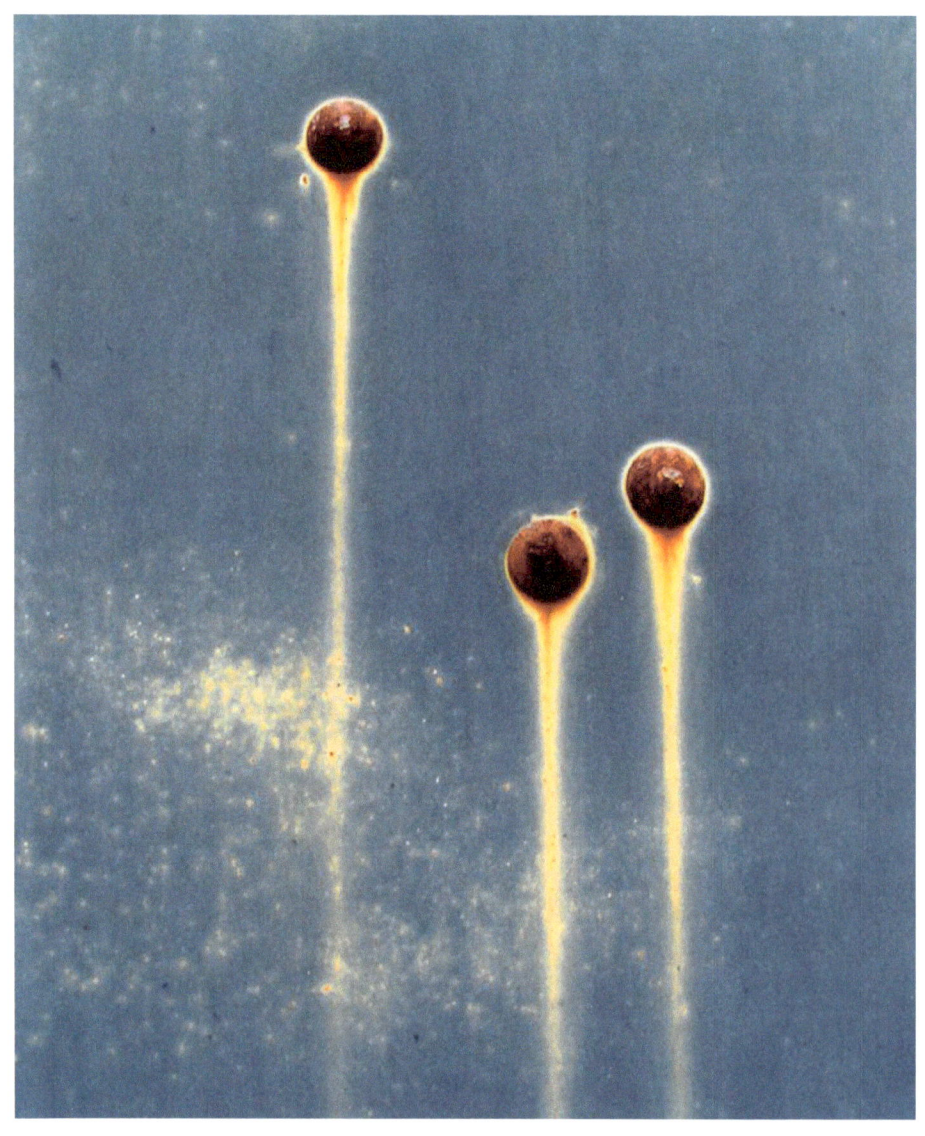

Autumn's Dance

Simply put,
I miss the
Days of
Cool and crisp
Autumn's time.
Short and swift
Passes the days
Until winter
Beats upon
The doorstep.

Colors abound
On boughs of
Sturdy oak trees,
Leaves color and curl,
Swirl and dance
To the cold and damp
Ground below.

Splendor in
Their days
They fall
To certain
Death
In whispering
Songs.

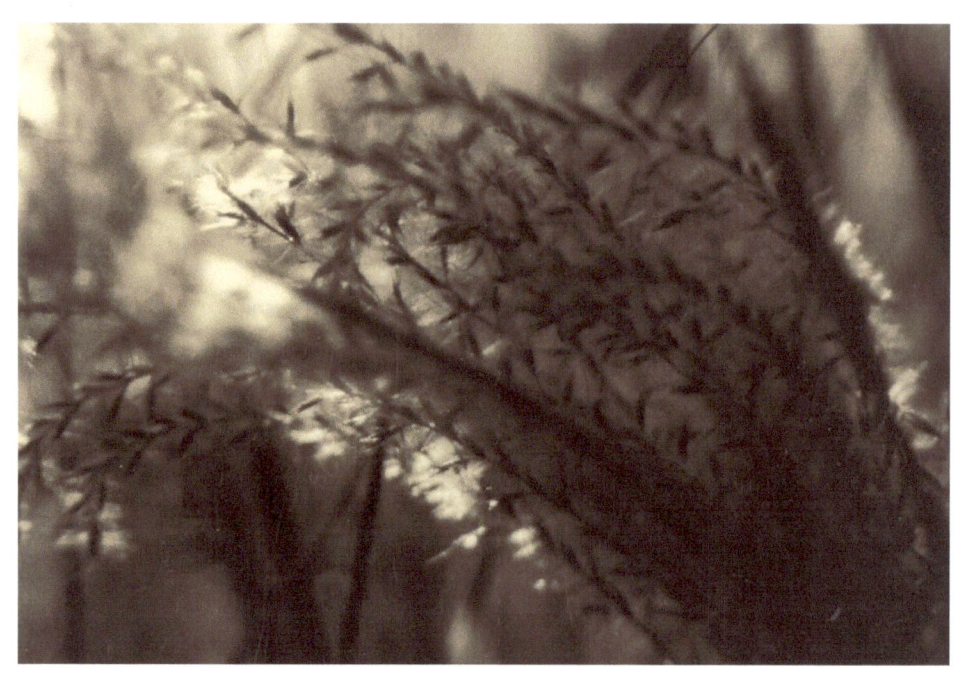

Love Song

Kisses are like the salt
To a bland diet.
Love is the lust
One seeks to
Alleviate boredom.

Today's bliss
Is
Yesterday's woe.

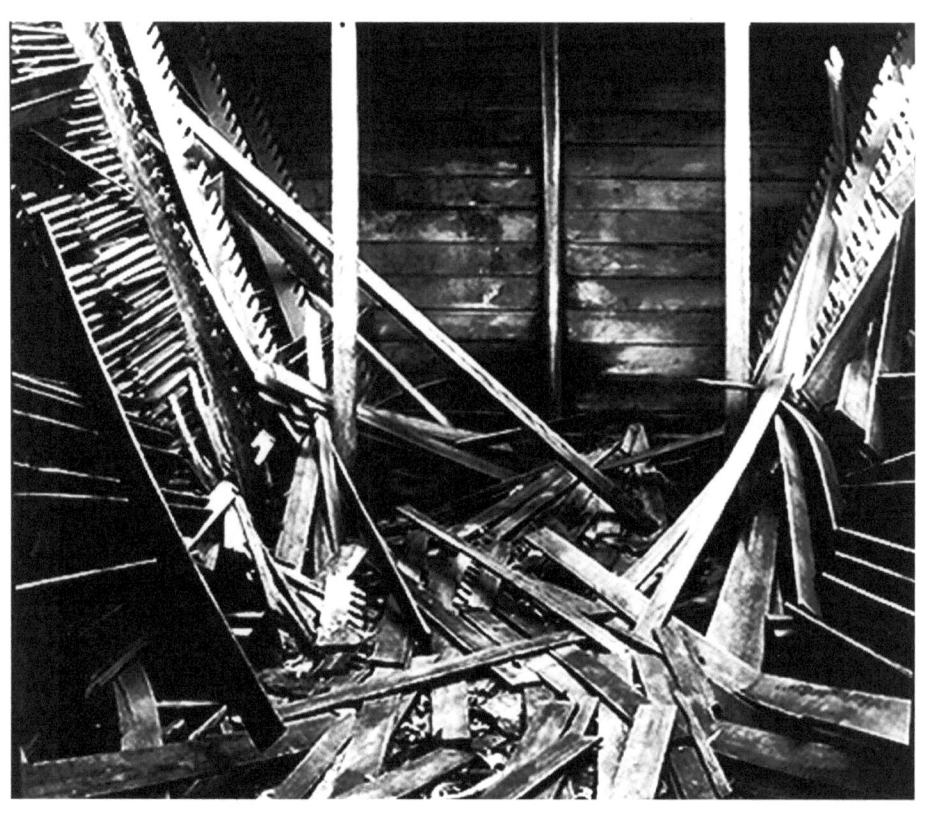

Regretfully Yours

Proposal

Apprehension.

Denial

Doubtfully submitted.

Inadvertently denied.

Painfully crushed.

On the rebound.

Regretfully yours,

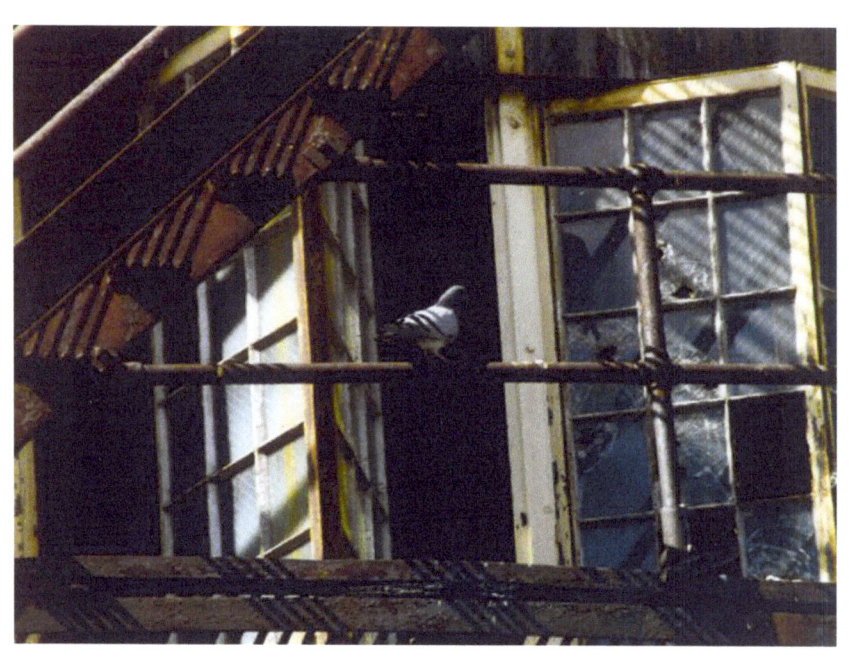

62

Virtual Romance

Young at heart
Pure in mind
Old in body.
Doesn't really matter
When a computer screen
Is your companion.
All that is unreal
Is somehow real
When stayed by the
Gentle beat of a heart
And the tap, tap, tap
Of the keyboard.
So can I cite
My not so real
Love for you.
All can be said
In a distance unfathomed
United by a modem
Disconnected by
Control
Alt
Delete.

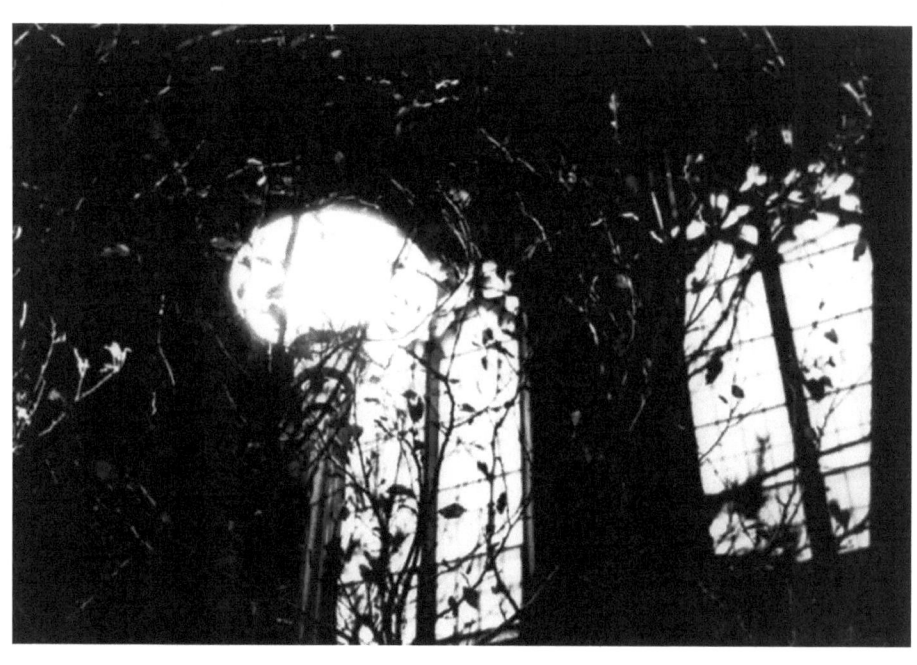

Sweet Rain

The distinct sound of thunder reminds of pending storm.
Spring flowers wait with anticipation of
gently, scented rain.
Flashes of lightening briefly
brighten in the cradled, blackened sky.
Squirrels chew on telephone wires
before making haste to
safety of shelter.
While birds search the grass for
light and tasty treats.
Welcome the rain,
enter spring time once again.
Sweet spring showers sing
upon the window pane,
dance on the rooftop,
keep the season in pace to
bring the promise of summer
with a musical approach.